Crockle T
a Swim

Written and Illustrated by

John Ryan

The sun was blazing down and it was a fine hot afternoon.

All around the Ark the water sparkled.

High above, the birds from the Ark flew merrily round and round

and all the people and the animals on board were making the most of the lovely weather.

At one end of the warm deck the animals, large and small, sprawled and slept happily.

At the other end, the family were all enjoying themselves in different ways.

Mrs Noah had brought her plants out to water them. Her youngest son Jaffet was playing deck-quoits with his friend Jannet.

And even gloomy Mr and Mrs Shem were doing their best to sunbathe.

Cheerful Mrs Ham was trying to catch fish for supper. They were all having a lot of fun – even though the quoit landed in the wrong place and Mrs Ham caught Mrs Shem's bonnet instead of a mackerel!

Crockle, the pet baby crocodile who shouldn't have been on the Ark at all, was sitting on the side looking at the cool water and longing to have a swim.

In fact the only people indoors were Mr Noah, who was busy painting a notice in his study,

and his son Ham the carpenter who was banging and hammering deep down inside the Ark. Nobody, except his father, knew exactly what he was up to.

When Jaffet and Jannet had finished their game they felt hot and tired. Like Crockle they wanted a swim. Then out came Mr Noah with his notice.

But when they asked him, Mr Noah said 'No'. He put up the notice. It said 'No Bathing'.

No Bathing
No!
But why?
But... but...
Now listen. However fierce the animals are on *board* the Ark, they all do what I say.
But out there under the deep water there are creatures who have nothing to do with the Ark. They are dangerous and I cannot control them.
Come down below.
If Ham has finished his work, you will understand better.

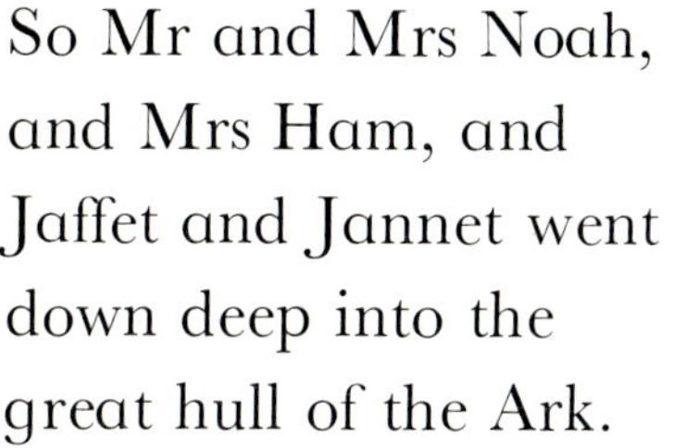

So Mr and Mrs Noah, and Mrs Ham, and Jaffet and Jannet went down deep into the great hull of the Ark.

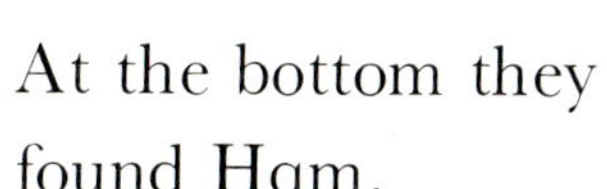

At the bottom they found Ham.

He was looking very pleased with himself. Then he showed them what he'd been doing.

He had built a great glass window in the side of the Ark below the level of the water. Through the window the family could see strange fishes gathering outside.

‘Goodness!’ said Jaffet, ‘I had no idea there were so many living things in the water.’ ‘There are a lot more than those,’ said Mr Noah. ‘Just watch!’ And as they watched, they saw . . .

flat fish and fat fish, saw-fish and sword-fish,

shellfish and jellyfish and a horrible ugly octopus.

Just then Mr and Mrs Shem came down.
'I've put a new mirror up,' said Ham. 'Take a look!'

When Mr and Mrs Shem looked in the glass they had a shock. There happened to be two very ugly fish looking in and Mr and Mrs Shem thought they were looking at themselves. Ham laughed. 'Don't worry, it isn't really a mirror,' he said. 'It's a window for looking out under the water.'

By this time some of the animals had come down to see what was going on. So the animals looked at the fishes,

and the fishes looked at the animals. They were all very surprised. None of them had ever seen anything like each other before!

Then Jaffet and Jannet suddenly saw something which wasn't a fish, or indeed any sort of sea creature.

It was Crockle! The naughty baby crocodile had waited until he was left all alone on deck, then he dived in to have a swim. And now he was showing off, outside the water-window!

'Come back, you bad crocodile!' shouted Jaffet. But Crockle couldn't hear him through the glass. Anyway he was enjoying himself too much

as he looped the loop

and did every kind of trick.

He was just doing a daring nose-dive when suddenly he looked up. A look of terror came over his face and a moment later he was off,

closely followed by an enormous shark! 'It'll gobble him up!' shouted Ham. 'What can we do to help?' cried Jaffet. 'Nothing down here,' said Mr Noah. 'All up on deck!'

So they all rushed up the stairs,

to try to save poor Crockle.

When everybody got up on deck

they saw that Crockle had reached the surface.

All they could see of the shark

was its big, dark, frightening fin

and it was getting closer . . .

and closer . . .

and closer.

Crockle was swimming for his life!

Ham seized a lifebelt. 'Don't throw it until I say,' ordered Mr Noah. 'And the rest of you . . . shout and roar and make as much noise as you can to distract the shark!'

So all the people and animals yelled and cheered and made a great noise. When the shark lifted its ugly head out of the water to put an end to Crockle, it was deafened. But Crockle was getting tired.

'Now!' shouted Noah, and Ham threw the lifebelt as hard and as far as he could towards the baby crocodile.

The shark was nearly there. Its sharp teeth were just about to close on Crockle.

But Ham's aim was good.

With a last desperate effort Crockle was just able to jump into the lifebelt.

Then with a mighty tug, Ham plucked it, Crockle and all, out of the water.

And the shark's great mouth snapped shut . . . on nothing!

Crockle was safe.

A moment later he was back on board again.

Then everybody made a fuss of him.

Mrs Ham gave him a bowl of tasty soup to make him strong.

Mrs Shem gave him a knitted scarf to keep him warm.

And even gloomy old Shem tickled his tummy.

Mr Noah usually pretended that Crockle wasn't there. He had two perfectly good (or bad) crocodiles on the Ark already. But now he patted him quite kindly on the head.

'After all, I did put up a notice saying No Bathing.'
'I know,' said Jaffet, 'but surely, Father. . .

‘even the cleverest baby crocodiles
can’t read!’